THE POETRY OF
YTTERBIUM

The Poetry of Ytterbium

Walter the Educator

Silent King Books a WhichHead Imprint

Copyright © 2024 by Walter the Educator

All rights reserved. No part of this book may be reproduced in any manner whatsoever without written permission except in the case of brief quotations embodied in critical articles and reviews.

First Printing, 2024

Disclaimer
This book is a literary work; poems are not about specific persons, locations, situations, and/or circumstances unless mentioned in a historical context. This book is for entertainment and informational purposes only. The author and publisher offer this information without warranties expressed or implied. No matter the grounds, neither the author nor the publisher will be accountable for any losses, injuries, or other damages caused by the reader's use of this book. The use of this book acknowledges an understanding and acceptance of this disclaimer.

"Earning a degree in chemistry changed my life!"
– Walter the Educator

dedicated to all the chemistry lovers, like myself, across the world

CONTENTS

Dedication v

Why I Created This Book? 1

One - Ytterbium, Oh Ytterbium 2

Two - Cannot Hide 4

Three - Distant Lands 6

Four - Ytterbium's Presence 8

Five - Masterpiece Of Art 10

Six - Catalyst For Innovation 12

Seven - Cosmic Mystery 14

Eight - Rare And Wondrous Form 16

Nine - Ytterbium's Allure 18

Ten - Honor Ytterbium 20

Eleven - Whisper Of Wonder 21

Twelve - Secrets They Entail 23

Thirteen - Masterpiece Of Science's Ar	...	25
Fourteen - Dance Of Atoms	....	26
Fifteen - Elemental Glory	....	27
Sixteen - Cosmic Connection	....	28
Seventeen - Ytterbium's Brilliance	....	30
Eighteen - Leave Your Mark	....	31
Nineteen - Jive	....	32
Twenty - Treasure Trove	....	34
Twenty-One - The Key	....	36
Twenty-Two - Find Your Stride	....	37
Twenty-Three - Celestial Display	......	39
Twenty-Four - Devices And Lasers	......	41
Twenty-Five - Scientific Artistry	......	42
Twenty-Six - Brightly Shine	....	44
Twenty-Seven - Cosmic Gem	....	46
Twenty-Eight - Ytterbium, In Your Mystique	......	48
Twenty-Nine - Cosmic Dream	....	50
Thirty - Presence Reigns	....	51
Thirty-One - Ancient Times To The Modern Age	....	52

Thirty-Two - Universe Adjourns 54

Thirty-Three - Intricate Domain 56

Thirty-Four - Number 70 58

Thirty-Five - Ytterbium Whispers 60

Thirty-Six - Ytterbium Echoes 62

Thirty-Seven - Corridors Of Time 64

About The Author 66

WHY I CREATED THIS BOOK?

Crafting a poetic anthology centered around the chemical element Ytterbium was an intriguing endeavor that unveils the artistic potential residing in scientific realms. The atomic allure of Ytterbium, with its atomic number 70 and unique spectral characteristics, provides a poetic canvas to explore the intricacies of the periodic table. Through verses and stanzas, one can delve into its electron configuration dance and the quantum choreography that defines its essence.

ONE

YTTERBIUM, OH YTTERBIUM

In the depths of the periodic table, obscure and rare,
Lies Ytterbium, a metal beyond compare.
Silvery and lustrous, it shines with brilliance untold,
A treasure of the earth, a marvel to behold.

Its atomic number sixty-nine, a prime in its own right,
Ytterbium's presence is a captivating sight.
It dances with electrons in its orbital shell,
A symphony of science that no words can truly tell.

From the mines of Sweden, its origin is traced,
A legacy of discovery, in time and space.
Its properties unique, its essence enigmatic,
Ytterbium beckons with a mystery so dramatic.

In lasers and alloys, its uses unfold,
A versatile element, with stories yet untold.

It whispers secrets of the universe, hidden in its core,
A cosmic connection that leaves us craving more.
  Ytterbium, oh Ytterbium, a marvel of creation,
A testament to nature's wondrous variation.
In the tapestry of elements, you shine with rare allure,
A timeless testament to the wonders we endure.
  So let us raise our voices in praise of this element grand,
Ytterbium, oh Ytterbium, in our hearts, you firmly stand.

TWO

CANNOT HIDE

Ytterbium, a treasure of the Earth's embrace,
Unveils its secrets, its enigmatic grace.
From the mines of Sweden, it emerged with pride,
A rare and wondrous metal, no secrets to hide.

In 1878, Marignac's keen eye discerned,
A new element from erbium, a lesson learned.
Ytterbium, the name he bestowed with care,
A tribute to Ytterby, a village so rare.

Soft and lustrous, its allure shines bright,
A malleable marvel, a radiant light.
Seven isotopes, stable and true,
Reveal the essence of Ytterbium's debut.

Dissolved by acids, yet resilient and bold,
Ytterbium's story in the annals of old.
A catalyst for change, in stainless steel it dwells,
A beacon of innovation, its tale it compels.

In memory devices and tuneable lasers it finds,
A purpose in progress, in the depths of our minds.
A whisper of wonder, a hint of the unknown,
Ytterbium's journey, in history it's sown.

So let us marvel at this element rare,
Ytterbium's legacy beyond compare.
In the tapestry of elements, it stands with pride,
A testament to nature's secrets, it cannot hide.

THREE

DISTANT LANDS

    Ytterbium, a shimmering mystery of sixty-nine,
A tale untold, a rare gem to define.
In the depths of the Earth, it quietly resides,
A silent witness to the universe's tides.
    From the mines of Sweden, it was brought to light,
A precious metal, gleaming pure and bright.
Marignac's keen insight, a discovery profound,
Unveiled Ytterbium, in science it was crowned.
    Soft and silvery, it dances with grace,
A symphony of atoms, in a cosmic embrace.
Malleable and precious, its atoms entwine,
Revealing the secrets of Ytterbium's design.
    In lasers it pulses, a beacon of light,
In atomic clocks, it measures time just right.
A catalyst for progress, in alloys it thrives,
Ytterbium's essence in innovation thrives.

A whisper of wonder, in the periodic chart,
Ytterbium's presence, a masterpiece of art.
In the fabric of elements, it weaves its tale,
A legacy of curiosity that will never pale.

So let us honor Ytterbium, in its rarest form,
A testament to nature's intricate norm.
In the grand symphony of the elements, it stands,
Ytterbium's allure, across distant lands.

FOUR

YTTERBIUM'S PRESENCE

Ytterbium, a jewel in the crown of the periodic table,
An enigma wrapped in atomic stability, an elemental fable.
Born from the Swedish earth, it emerged with silent grace,
A testament to nature's ingenuity, a rare and precious embrace.

Atomic number sixty-nine, a prime among its peers,
Ytterbium's presence, a symphony that resonates and adheres.
Silvery and lustrous, its atoms entwine and dance,
A cosmic ballet of elements, a tale of chance.

Marignac's discerning eye, in 1878, unveiled its hidden guise,

A discovery that echoed through scientific skies.
Soft and malleable, yet resilient in its core,
Ytterbium's essence, a testament to the Earth's ancient lore.

In lasers and atomic clocks, its purpose comes to light,
A beacon of precision, in the depths of scientific might.
A catalyst for innovation, in alloys it finds its role,
Ytterbium's legacy, a testament to the elements' grand parole.

So let us marvel at Ytterbium, in its rare and wondrous form,
A cosmic connection, a treasure in the elemental storm.
In the grand tapestry of creation, it stands with rare allure,
Ytterbium's presence, a symphony of elements, forever to endure.

FIVE

MASTERPIECE OF ART

In the heart of Earth's embrace, a treasure was found,
Ytterbium, a jewel of the periodic table, renowned.
Marignac's discerning eye, in eighteen seventy-eight,
Unveiled its presence, a discovery so great.
　Soft and silvery, its atoms entwine and play,
A dance of elements, in a cosmic array.
Malleable and precious, its essence unfolds,
Ytterbium's story, in the annals of old.
　In lasers and atomic clocks, it finds its place,
A beacon of precision, in the vast expanse of space.
A catalyst for progress, in alloys it thrives,
Ytterbium's legacy, in the tapestry of lives.
　So let us honor Ytterbium, in its rarest form,
A testament to nature's intricate norm.

In the grand symphony of elements, it stands,
Ytterbium's allure, across distant lands.
    In the tapestry of creation, it weaves its tale,
A legacy of curiosity that will never pale.
A whisper of wonder, in the periodic chart,
Ytterbium's presence, a masterpiece of art.

SIX

CATALYST FOR INNOVATION

Ytterbium, oh element divine,
In the periodic table, your place does shine.
A lustrous metal, in the Earth's deep hold,
Your story unfolds, a tale so bold.

Hailing from Swedish mines, your journey began,
A discovery that echoed through the scientific span.
Soft and silvery, yet resilient and strong,
In the world of elements, you truly belong.

In lasers and atomic clocks, your presence is seen,
A symbol of precision, in the scientific scene.
A catalyst for innovation, in alloys you thrive,
Ytterbium, in the grand tapestry of elements, you strive.

So let us celebrate Ytterbium, a marvel so rare,
A testament to nature's wondrous, intricate affair.

In the cosmic dance of atoms, you play your part,
Ytterbium's essence, a masterpiece of art.
    In the grand symphony of creation, you hold your sway,
Ytterbium, in your elemental glory, you stay.
A whisper of wonder, in the scientific chart,
Ytterbium's presence, forever a work of art.

SEVEN

COSMIC MYSTERY

In the realm of atomic wonders, you hold your place,
Ytterbium, a marvel of the cosmic race.
In lasers and atomic clocks, your essence is found,
A beacon of precision, in the scientific ground.

A catalyst for progress, in alloys you reside,
Ytterbium, in the grand symphony, you glide.
So let us marvel at your rare and wondrous form,
A testament to nature's intricate norm.

In the tapestry of elements, you weave your tale,
Ytterbium's presence, a masterpiece beyond the pale.
A whisper of wonder, in the periodic chart,
Ytterbium's allure, a symphony of science's art.

In the grand design of creation, you stand with pride,
Ytterbium, in your elemental glory, you abide.

A testament to nature's secrets, you hold the key,
Ytterbium, in your enigma, a cosmic mystery.

EIGHT

RARE AND WONDROUS FORM

Ytterbium, in the depths of the periodic table you reside,
A silent sentinel, in the grand cosmic tide.
In atomic clocks, your precision marks the beat,
Ytterbium, in the fabric of elements, your role is replete.

A catalyst for progress, in lasers you shine,
Ytterbium, in the realm of science, you define.
A whisper of wonder, in the annals of old,
Ytterbium's story, in mysteries untold.

So let us pay homage to your rare and wondrous form,
A testament to nature's intricate norm.
In the grand orchestra of creation, you play your part,

Ytterbium's essence, a masterpiece of the elemental art.

In the cosmic dance of atoms, your dance is sublime,
Ytterbium, in your enigma, you mark the time.
A beacon of innovation, in alloys you thrive,
Ytterbium's legacy, in the tapestry of lives.

So here's to Ytterbium, in your cosmic mystery,
A testament to the wonders of chemistry.
In the grand symphony of elements, you stand,
Ytterbium's allure, across the distant lands.

NINE

YTTERBIUM'S ALLURE

Ytterbium, oh Ytterbium, a rare and wondrous sight,
In the realm of elements, you shimmer with delight.
In the grand cosmic dance, you hold a mystic sway,
Ytterbium, in your essence, you lead the way.

A catalyst for progress, in lasers you find your voice,
Ytterbium's legacy, a testament to our choice.
In the fabric of creation, you weave a tale so bright,
Ytterbium's presence, a symphony of light.

So let us honor Ytterbium, in its rarest form,
A cosmic connection, a treasure in the elemental storm.
In the grand tapestry of elements, it stands,
Ytterbium's allure, across distant lands.

A whisper of wonder, in the periodic chart,
Ytterbium's essence, a masterpiece of art.

In memory devices and tuneable lasers you reside,
Ytterbium, in your splendor, you cannot hide.

TEN

HONOR YTTERBIUM

In the cosmic tapestry, your presence is felt,
Ytterbium, a marvel of creation, in which we have dwelt.
A testament to nature's wondrous variation,
In the dance of elements, you hold fascination.

In the symphony of atoms, your melody plays,
Ytterbium, in your enigma, you continue to amaze.
A beacon of innovation, in alloys you thrive,
Ytterbium's legacy, in the tapestry of lives.

So let us honor Ytterbium, in its rare and intricate form,
A cosmic connection, a treasure in the elemental storm.
In the grand design of creation, you hold your sway,
Ytterbium, in your elemental glory, you forever stay.

ELEVEN

WHISPER OF WONDER

Ytterbium, in your radiant allure,
A testament to nature's secrets, so pure.
In the cosmic dance of elements, you hold your place,
Ytterbium's presence, a marvel of grace.

In the grand symphony of creation, you stand tall,
Ytterbium, in your enigmatic sprawl.
A whisper of wonder, in the periodic chart,
Ytterbium's essence, a masterpiece of art.

In memory devices and tuneable lasers, you find your role,
Ytterbium, in your brilliance, a treasure to extol.
A beacon of innovation, in alloys you shine,
Ytterbium's legacy, a testament so fine.

So here's to Ytterbium, in its rare and wondrous form,
A cosmic connection, a treasure in the elemental

norm.
In the grand tapestry of elements, it weaves its tale,
Ytterbium's allure, a symphony that will never pale.

TWELVE

SECRETS THEY ENTAIL

    Ytterbium, a gem in the periodic table's domain,
A marvel of chemistry, in its enigmatic reign.
In the cosmic symphony of elements, it holds its ground,
Ytterbium's allure, a treasure to be found.
    A beacon of innovation, in lasers it finds its role,
Ytterbium's legacy, a testament to the elements' grand parole.
In the grand tapestry of creation, it weaves its tale,
Ytterbium's presence, a masterpiece beyond the pale.
    So let us honor Ytterbium, in its rare and wondrous form,
A cosmic connection, a treasure in the elemental storm.
In the grand design of the universe, it plays its part,
Ytterbium's essence, a symphony of science's art.

In the dance of atoms and the secrets they entail,
Ytterbium, in your enigma, you never fail.
A whisper of wonder, in the scientific chart,
Ytterbium's allure, a symphony of nature's art.

THIRTEEN

MASTERPIECE OF SCIENCE'S AR

Ytterbium, in your rarity, you hold allure,
A beacon of innovation, a treasure to secure.
In the grand tapestry of elements, you stand tall,
Ytterbium's presence, a marvel to enthrall.

A testament to nature's intricate design,
Ytterbium, in your essence, you forever shine.
In the cosmic symphony of creation, you play your part,
Ytterbium's allure, a masterpiece of science's art.

In the fabric of elements, you weave your tale,
Ytterbium, in your enigma, you'll never pale.
A whisper of wonder, in the periodic chart,
Ytterbium's presence, a symphony to impart.

FOURTEEN

DANCE OF ATOMS

Ytterbium, in your rarity, a marvel to behold,
A testament to the universe's secrets untold.
In the grand tapestry of elements, you hold your sway,
Ytterbium's allure, a masterpiece to convey.

In the dance of atoms and their intricate chore,
Ytterbium, in your enigma, you explore.
A whisper of wonder, in the scientific chart,
Ytterbium's presence, a symphony of nature's art.

FIFTEEN

ELEMENTAL GLORY

Ytterbium, in your rare and precious form,
A testament to nature's intricate norm.
In the grand design of the elements, you hold your sway,
Ytterbium's allure, a masterpiece to convey.

In the cosmic ballet of atoms, you play your part,
Ytterbium's essence, a treasure close to heart.
A whisper of wonder, in the periodic chart,
Ytterbium's presence, a symphony to impart.

In the grand tapestry of creation, you leave your mark,
Ytterbium, in your elemental glory, a cosmic spark.
A testament to nature's secrets, you hold the key,
Ytterbium, in your enigma, a marvel for all to see.

SIXTEEN

COSMIC CONNECTION

Ytterbium, in your atomic dance, you gracefully twirl,
A marvel to behold, a gem in the elemental swirl.
In the grand design of the universe, you claim your place,
Ytterbium's allure, a testament to cosmic grace.

In the symphony of elements, you hold a special role,
Ytterbium, in your enigmatic nature, you console.
A whisper of wonder, in the scientific chart,
Ytterbium's presence, a symphony to impart.

In the cosmic dance of atoms, you shine bright,
Ytterbium, in your elemental form, a radiant light.
A testament to nature's wonders, you stand tall,
Ytterbium, in your enduring splendor, you enthrall.

So here's to Ytterbium, a marvel in the grand

scheme,
A cosmic connection, a treasure beyond a dream.
In the fabric of creation, you weave your tale,
Ytterbium's essence, a masterpiece beyond the pale.

SEVENTEEN

YTTERBIUM'S BRILLIANCE

Ytterbium, a luminescent gem in the grand design,
In the cosmic dance of elements, you brightly shine.
A testament to nature's secrets, you hold the key,
Ytterbium, in your enigma, a marvel for all to see.

In the symphony of atoms and their intricate play,
Ytterbium, in your essence, you forever stay.
A whisper of wonder, in the periodic chart,
Ytterbium's allure, a symphony to impart.

So here's to Ytterbium, in its rare and wondrous form,
A cosmic connection, a treasure in the elemental norm.
In the grand tapestry of elements, it weaves its tale,
Ytterbium's brilliance, a gem that will never pale.

EIGHTEEN

LEAVE YOUR MARK

Ytterbium, in your enigmatic embrace,
A marvel in the grand cosmic space.
In the symphony of elements, you hold your ground,
Ytterbium's allure, a treasure to be found.

A beacon of innovation, in your atomic dance,
Ytterbium's legacy, a tale of chance.
In the fabric of creation, you leave your mark,
Ytterbium, in your elemental spark.

So here's to Ytterbium, in its rare and wondrous form,
A cosmic connection, a gem beyond the norm.
In the grand design of the universe, you play your part,
Ytterbium's essence, a masterpiece of science's art.

NINETEEN

JIVE

Ytterbium, in your enigmatic allure,
A cosmic treasure, so bright and pure.
In the grand tapestry of elements, you hold your place,
Ytterbium's essence, a marvel in space.

A whisper of wonder, in the periodic chart,
Ytterbium's presence, a symphony to impart.
A testament to nature's secrets, you shine so bright,
Ytterbium, in your rare form, a celestial light.

So here's to Ytterbium, a jewel in the elemental array,
A cosmic connection, a treasure that will forever stay.
In the dance of atoms and their intricate chore,
Ytterbium, in your enigma, you explore.

A beacon of innovation, in alloys you thrive,
Ytterbium's legacy, in the symphony of elements,

you jive.
In memory devices and tuneable lasers, you reside,
Ytterbium, in your splendor, you cannot hide.

TWENTY

TREASURE TROVE

Ytterbium, in your atomic embrace, a celestial dance unfolds,
A treasure trove of wonders, in your essence, it beholds.
In the cosmic symphony of elements, you hold your place,
Ytterbium's allure, a marvel to embrace.

In the web of creation, you weave a tale untold,
Ytterbium, in your enigma, a cosmic secret to behold.
A whisper of wonder, in the scientific chart,
Ytterbium's presence, a symphony to impart.

In the tapestry of atoms, your radiance shines bright,
Ytterbium, in your elemental form, a celestial light.
In the grand design of the universe, you play your

part,
Ytterbium's essence, a masterpiece of nature's art.

So here's to Ytterbium, a gem in the elemental array,
A cosmic connection, a treasure that will forever stay.
In memory devices and lasers, you find your stride,
Ytterbium, in your splendor, you cannot hide.

TWENTY-ONE

THE KEY

    Ytterbium, in your atomic dance, a cosmic delight,
A treasure of the periodic table, shining so bright.
In the symphony of elements, you hold your sway,
Ytterbium's allure, a marvel in the grand display.

    In the tapestry of creation, you leave your mark,
Ytterbium, in your enigmatic essence, a celestial spark.
A whisper of wonder, in the scientific chart,
Ytterbium's presence, a symphony to impart.

    In memory devices and lasers, you find your place,
Ytterbium, in your radiance, a celestial grace.
A testament to nature's secrets, you hold the key,
Ytterbium, in your allure, a marvel for all to see.

TWENTY-TWO

FIND YOUR STRIDE

Ytterbium, in your atomic dance, a cosmic ballet,
A testament to nature's wonders, you hold sway.
In the grand design of the universe, you play your part,
Ytterbium's allure, a symphony of science's art.

A whisper of wonder, in the periodic chart,
Ytterbium's presence, a masterpiece to impart.
A cosmic connection, a treasure beyond compare,
Ytterbium, in your essence, a marvel to declare.

In the fabric of elements, you weave your tale,
Ytterbium, in your enigma, you'll never pale.
A beacon of innovation, in your alloys you thrive,
Ytterbium's legacy, in the symphony of elements, you jive.

So here's to Ytterbium, a gem in the elemental array,
A cosmic connection, a treasure that will forever stay.

In memory devices and lasers, you find your stride,
Ytterbium, in your splendor, you cannot hide.

TWENTY-THREE

CELESTIAL DISPLAY

Ytterbium, in the cosmic dance, you hold your ground,
A rare gem in the periodic table, so profound.
In the symphony of elements, you play your part,
Ytterbium's allure, a masterpiece from the heart.

A whisper of wonder, in the scientific chart,
Ytterbium's presence, a symphony to impart.
In the fabric of creation, you leave your mark,
Ytterbium, in your elemental spark.

A beacon of innovation, in your alloys you thrive,
Ytterbium's legacy, in the grand cosmic hive.
In memory devices and lasers, you find your place,
Ytterbium, in your radiance, a celestial grace.

So here's to Ytterbium, a treasure of the cosmic array,
A cosmic connection, in the grand celestial display.

In the grand design of the universe, you play your part,
Ytterbium's essence, a masterpiece of science's art.

TWENTY-FOUR

DEVICES AND LASERS

Ytterbium, in your elemental form, a celestial light,
A testament to nature's secrets, you shine so bright.
In the grand tapestry of creation, you leave your mark,
Ytterbium, in your enduring splendor, you enthrall.

In the symphony of elements, you dance with grace,
Ytterbium's allure, a masterpiece of cosmic embrace.
A beacon of innovation, in your alloys you thrive,
Ytterbium's legacy, in the grand cosmic hive.

So here's to Ytterbium, a gem in the elemental array,
A cosmic connection, a treasure that will forever stay.
In memory devices and lasers, you find your place,
Ytterbium, in your radiance, a celestial grace.

TWENTY-FIVE

SCIENTIFIC ARTISTRY

Ytterbium, within your atomic dance, a cosmic delight,
In the tapestry of elements, you shine so bright,
A celestial gem, in the symphony of the periodic chart.

In the quantum world, your mysteries unfurl,
Ytterbium, in your essence, a cosmic pearl,
A treasure trove of scientific artistry, you impart.

In lasers and atomic clocks, your prowess is clear,
Ytterbium, in your radiance, you steer,
A cosmic navigator, guiding humanity's quest.

In the grand cosmic orchestra, you play your part,
Ytterbium's legacy, a masterpiece of nature's art,
A celestial enigma, forever to be addressed.

So here's to Ytterbium, in the cosmic array,
A cosmic connection that will forever stay,

In the dance of the cosmos, you hold a celestial place,
Ytterbium, in your elegance, a marvel to embrace.

TWENTY-SIX

BRIGHTLY SHINE

Ytterbium, in your enigmatic form, a celestial delight,
In the cosmic tapestry, you shimmer and ignite,
A stellar enigma, a spectacle to behold,
In the grand celestial dance, a story you've told.

In lasers and atomic clocks, your essence is found,
Ytterbium, in your radiance, the universe is bound,
A cosmic connection, in the elemental array,
The mystery of your existence, a cosmic ballet.

So here's to Ytterbium, in the grand cosmic scheme,
A celestial treasure, like a mesmerizing dream,
In the cosmic symphony, you play your part,
Ytterbium's essence, a masterpiece of scientific art.

In the grand cosmic puzzle, you hold a place,
Ytterbium, in your elegance, a celestial embrace,

A testament to nature's wonders, you brightly shine,
Ytterbium, in your brilliance, a cosmic design.

TWENTY-SEVEN

COSMIC GEM

Ytterbium, a cosmic gem, you hold the cosmic key,
In the grand celestial dance, you shimmer and you gleam,
A mysterious element, in the cosmic tapestry,
Ytterbium, in your essence, a celestial beam.

In the realm of science, you carve a wondrous path,
Ytterbium, in your splendor, a celestial aftermath,
A treasure of the cosmos, a marvel to behold,
Ytterbium, in your radiance, a story to be told.

So here's to Ytterbium, a celestial delight,
A cosmic connection, in the vast cosmic flight,
In the grand design of the universe, you play your part,
Ytterbium's essence, a masterpiece of science's art.

In the symphony of elements, you sing your unique song,

Ytterbium, in your enigma, you eternally belong,
A celestial wonder, in the cosmic expanse,
Ytterbium, in your allure, a cosmic dance.

TWENTY-EIGHT

YTTERBIUM, IN YOUR MYSTIQUE

Ytterbium, in your enigmatic grace,
A cosmic treasure in the vast celestial space,
In the grand cosmic orchestra, you hold a key,
Ytterbium, in your radiance, a marvel to see.

A beacon of innovation, in the symphony of elements, you thrive,
Ytterbium's legacy, in the grand cosmic hive,
In memory devices and lasers, you find your place,
Ytterbium, in your brilliance, a celestial embrace.

So here's to Ytterbium, a gem in the elemental array,
A cosmic connection, a treasure that will forever stay,
In the grand design of the universe, you play your part,
Ytterbium's essence, a masterpiece of nature's art.

A testament to nature's secrets, you proudly stand,

Ytterbium, in your allure, a marvel of the cosmic grand,
In the cosmic dance of elements, you elegantly twirl,
Ytterbium, in your mystique, a celestial pearl.

TWENTY-NINE

COSMIC DREAM

Ytterbium, a celestial jewel in the cosmic array,
In the grand design of the universe, you beautifully sway,
A treasure of science, in your atomic choreography,
Ytterbium, in your elegance, a celestial symphony.

In the cosmic dance of elements, you gracefully glide,
Ytterbium, in your enigma, you never hide,
A cosmic connection, in the grand cosmic play,
Ytterbium, in your radiance, a celestial display.

In lasers and devices, your essence is found,
Ytterbium, in your brilliance, a celestial crown,
A testament to nature's artistry, you brightly gleam,
Ytterbium, in your allure, a cosmic dream.

THIRTY

PRESENCE REIGNS

Ytterbium, a celestial gem, in the cosmic array,
A cosmic connection, in the grand celestial ballet,
In the symphony of elements, you hold a place,
Ytterbium's essence, a masterpiece of the cosmic grace.

In the dance of the universe, you elegantly sway,
Ytterbium, in your radiance, a celestial display,
A testament to nature's wonders, you brightly shine,
Ytterbium, in your allure, a cosmic design.

In memory devices and lasers, your presence reigns,
Ytterbium, in your brilliance, a celestial gains,
A cosmic enigma, forever to be explored,
Ytterbium, in your mystique, a celestial reward.

THIRTY-ONE

ANCIENT TIMES TO THE MODERN AGE

Ytterbium, a wondrous element of lore,
In the periodic table, it does implore.
With seventy protons, it takes its stand,
A shining gem in the alchemist's hand.

Its silvery gleam, a sight to behold,
In the Earth's embrace, its secrets unfold.
Rare and precious, it quietly resides,
In the realm of elements, it abides.

Ytterbium, with its magnetic allure,
In the laboratory, its mysteries endure.
A conductor of light, in lasers it thrives,
In the world of science, it bravely drives.

From ancient times to the modern age,
Ytterbium's tale turns a captivating page.

In communication and technology's embrace,
It plays a role with elegance and grace.

Ytterbium, a symbol of ingenuity and might,
In the symphony of elements, it takes flight.
Its presence, a testament to human quest,
In the grand design, it stands the test.

So here's to Ytterbium, noble and rare,
In the cosmos of elements, it's beyond compare.
With its own story and unique charm,
In the tapestry of elements, it leaves its warm.

THIRTY-TWO

UNIVERSE ADJOURNS

In the realm of elements rare,
There lies Ytterbium, beyond compare.
A lustrous metal, with atomic number 70,
Its properties, a marvel of chemistry.

Ytterbium, a silent sentinel of the periodic table,
Shrouded in mystery, its secrets unstable.
Its magnetic allure, a captivating dance,
Drawing in curious minds with a magnetic trance.

A metal of intrigue, with a silvery hue,
Ytterbium's essence, a tantalizing debut.
With its high density and softness supreme,
It weaves a tale of wonder, like a mesmerizing dream.

In the depths of the earth, where treasures lay,
Ytterbium hides, in a mystical display.
A conductor of electricity, a conductor of light,
Illuminating pathways, in the cover of night.

Ytterbium, oh enigmatic element divine,
Your presence in the universe, a celestial sign.
From distant stars to the core of our being,
Your enigma and allure, forever unseeing.

So here's to Ytterbium, a marvel untold,
In the alchemy of nature, your secrets unfold.
A symphony of protons, electrons, and neutrons,
In Ytterbium's embrace, the universe adjourns.

THIRTY-THREE

INTRICATE DOMAIN

Ytterbium, element of mystique profound,
In the tapestry of elements, rarely found.
With atomic number 70, a treasure untold,
Its story in the cosmos, waiting to unfold.

A silvery metal, with luster so bright,
Ytterbium's essence, a celestial light.
In the crucible of stars, where elements form,
Ytterbium dances, in a cosmic storm.

Its magnetic allure, a captivating force,
Drawing in explorers on a celestial course.
Soft and malleable, yet with strength untold,
Ytterbium's secrets, a mystery to behold.

In the depths of the Earth, where treasures lie,
Ytterbium slumbers, out of mortal eye.
A conductor of electricity, a beacon of might,
Ytterbium's whispers, in the still of night.

Oh Ytterbium, enigmatic element divine,
In the alchemy of creation, your wonders shine.
From quantum realms to the expanse of space,
Ytterbium's symphony, a cosmic embrace.

So here's to Ytterbium, in its silent refrain,
A testament to nature's intricate domain.
In the grand design of the universe's scheme,
Ytterbium's enigma, a celestial dream.

THIRTY-FOUR

NUMBER 70

Ytterbium, rare and serene,
In the depths of the periodic scene.
With atomic number 70, it reigns,
Amidst the elements, it sustains.

A lustrous metal, silvery and bright,
In its presence, all seems just right.
Its properties, unique and profound,
In the world of elements, it astounds.

Ytterbium, in the Earth's crust it hides,
A treasure sought by ambitious tides.
From ores and minerals, it is derived,
In the hands of science, it has thrived.

Its magnetic allure, a marvel to behold,
In the laboratory, its mysteries unfold.
With a stable isotope, it holds its ground,
In the realm of elements, it is renowned.

Ytterbium, in lasers it finds its use,
In communication, it holds the truce.
Its presence in technology, a boon,
In the world of elements, it sings its tune.

Ytterbium, a symbol of rarity and grace,
In the pantheon of elements, it finds its place.
With its own story and unique charm,
In the tapestry of elements, it leaves its warm.

Ytterbium, a muse for the curious mind,
In the realm of elements, it is one of a kind.

THIRTY-FIVE

YTTERBIUM WHISPERS

In the realm of elements, Ytterbium resides,
A luminescent dance where secrets often hide.
Atomic number seventy, its essence pure,
A symphony of particles, mysterious allure.

    Beneath the periodic table's coded script,
Ytterbium's saga, quietly equipped.
Rare earth whispers echo in its core,
A tale of electrons, an elemental lore.

    Silent symphony, a dance of sixty-nine,
Protons in tandem, a celestial design.
Neutrons join the cosmic waltz,
Gravity's caress, in quantum exalts.

    Ytterbium's luminescence in quantum strings,
A phosphorescent ballet that the cosmos brings.

Electron clouds twirl in vibrant arrays,
A dance of valence, where energy plays.
    Noble Ytterbium, in the celestial ballet,
A stellar performance in the atomic display.
Transitioning states, in spectral attire,
Elements entwined, a celestial choir.
    In the alchemy of creation, Ytterbium's embrace,
A stellar ballet in the cosmic space.
So in the elements' grand, cosmic rhyme,
Ytterbium whispers its secrets through time.

THIRTY-SIX

YTTERBIUM ECHOES

Within the tapestry of the periodic table's domain,
Ytterbium emerges, a luminescent refrain.
Atomic waltz of protons, in quantum parade,
A clandestine ballet in the cosmic arcade.

　　Electron ballet, a dance of seventy in tandem,
Orbiting tales spun, a celestial anthem.
In the nucleus, a symphony of particles bind,
Ytterbium's essence, a secret, enigmatic find.

　　A rare-earth minuet, whispers of sixty-nine,
Neutrons harmonize in the quantum design.
Noble Ytterbium, with atomic grace,
A radiant tapestry in the elemental space.

　　Phosphorescent hues paint the atomic stage,
Valence electrons pirouette in a vibrant cage.

The alchemy of Ytterbium, a cosmic charade,
Mystical transitions in the quantum cascade.
    A stellar masquerade, its secrets untold,
Ytterbium's story in the celestial scroll.
A dance of elements in the cosmic rhyme,
Ytterbium, the luminescent whisper through time.
    So, in the cosmic theater, Ytterbium performs,
A radiant ballet, where each atom transforms.
In the grand tapestry of the elemental chime,
Ytterbium echoes, an enigmatic paradigm.

THIRTY-SEVEN

CORRIDORS OF TIME

In the elemental tapestry where mysteries twine,
Ytterbium emerges, a luminescent sign.
Protons and neutrons in a cosmic dance,
Atomic number seventy, a quantum trance.

Within the nucleus, a celestial ballet,
Ytterbium's secret, in the atomic array.
Rare-earth whispers echo, a cryptic theme,
A dance of particles in the quantum stream.

Electrons pirouette, their valence embrace,
Ytterbium's choreography, an intricate grace.
Phosphorescent hues adorn the atomic stage,
A radiant minuet, in the elemental page.

Silent transitions in the quantum tide,
Ytterbium's secrets, where particles hide.
A noble element in the periodic rhyme,
A luminescent saga, unfolding through time.

Through the cosmic ballet, Ytterbium weaves,
A symphony of particles, as the universe conceives.
In the stellar theater, an atomic mime,
Ytterbium whispers, an enigmatic paradigm.

So, in the grand dance of elements untold,
Ytterbium's story in quantum unfold.
A celestial minuet, a luminescent rhyme,
Ytterbium's dance through the corridors of time.

ABOUT THE AUTHOR

Walter the Educator is one of the pseudonyms for Walter Anderson. Formally educated in Chemistry, Business, and Education, he is an educator, an author, a diverse entrepreneur, and he is the son of a disabled war veteran. "Walter the Educator" shares his time between educating and creating. He holds interests and owns several creative projects that entertain, enlighten, enhance, and educate, hoping to inspire and motivate you.

Follow, find new works, and stay up to date with Walter the Educator™ at WaltertheEducator.com

www.ingramcontent.com/pod-product-compliance
Lightning Source LLC
LaVergne TN
LVHW052002060526
838201LV00059B/3786